DESTINY

JEFFREY L. VANDE VOORT

The characters and events in this book are fictitious. Any similarities to actual persons, whether living or dead, are coincidental and not intended by the author. This book was written for informational purposes only. This book should not replace or take precedence over expert advice.

Copyright © 2023 Jeffrey L. Vande Voort All rights reserved.

No part of this work may be reproduced, stored in a retrieval system, or transmitted in any form or by any means, electronic, mechanical, photocopying, recording, scanning, or otherwise, without the author's prior written permission. Requests should be emailed to oatmeal.and.bibs@gmail.com.

Definitions cited in the preface are from Oxford Languages, Oxford University Press, 2023.
The author's photograph was taken by his daughter.
The artwork in this document, including the front and back covers, was arranged and painted by the Author using Krita 5.1.5 Software (2007).

Second Edition.
10 9 8 7 6 5 4 3 2

Destiny

Noun / des-ti-ny

• The events that will necessarily happen to a particular person or thing in the future.

• The hidden power believed to control what will happen in the future, fate.

- Oxford Languages

Chapter 1

Theo stared at his computer screen, waiting for just the right moment. His best friend, Elliot, listened on the other side of their internet phone. "Elliot, run your warrior through the front gate," Theo said. They were playing *Hillside Warriors*, a multi-player computer game known for mixing old fort designs with state-of-the-art sniper rifles. Theo and Elliot were a team. As soldiers of fortune, their mission was to invade guardian territories and cash in as much gold as possible. The fort had a lot of gold, and they were going after it.

Elliot's warrior entered the fort, sliding quickly past the entrance. Hiding behind a pole, his warrior searched for other defending guardians. Not recognizing any movement, Elliot yells over his phone, "It's all clear. Come on in." The old fort was built between two rolling hills next to a river. Theo lay on an outer hill watching for movement on the fort's walkways and parapets, but all was quiet.

Theo sarcastically asked, "So, you don't need my expert marksmanship?"

"I am way ahead of you. I killed the only defending guardian with one shot."

"I'm coming in," Theo said, running his warrior over the drawbridge and through the gate. "Now we just need to find the gold." Both heard a loud bang as Theo's player began to fall over. "I thought you shot them all."

"Oops. They were waiting on the other side of the fort. I didn't see them until they fired the shot." Elliot swung his rifle around, firing at the guardian. "I got him. He's gone."

'I am waiting,' Theo thought as he was kicked out of the game. "We'll hurry up. This game's home page is boring. I might start the next game without you."

"No, don't. Just sit there and wait. Think about solving world peace or something."

He put on his shoes instead. They continued playing while chatting back and forth on their phones. After a little while, Theo heard a knock at his bedroom door. "Come in," he said.

Ella, his girlfriend, walked in the door. She was wearing a tight white polo, white shorts, white socks, and white shoes. Her teeth were even whitened. Her hair was pulled back into a tight ponytail, revealing her forehead glowing with lotion. Sitting on Theo's bed, she began texting her friend. It was a beautiful Saturday afternoon, and they planned to play tennis at Bloomington Park, only a few blocks north of their houses. The park had a spray pad, several playgrounds, a larger shelter building, and tennis courts. The park's sandy beach next to West Lake was a favorite swimming spot that they had enjoyed since she could remember. Ella noticed that Theo had his socks and shoes on.

"My bike is outside. Are you ready?" she said.

He didn't look up from the monitor. "In a minute," Theo said. She was being ignored again. She looked around Theo's room. His room was a cluttered mess. Last night's fast-food bag was sitting on the wastebasket rim, waiting to be jammed in. His bed sheets were draped over the edge of the bed. His clothes from yesterday had missed the laundry basket. She wanted to clean it up, but instead, she texted her mother: *I have to tell him.*

"That bastard!" Theo shouted after being killed by another guardian. Elliot started laughing over the phone. Ella smiled.

Theo began to pick up the keyboard when she told him, "Stop! Put it down before you break it. It's time to go play tennis."

He put it down with a loud bang anyway as he said, "You're right, love. Let's go play tennis."

Strolling out of the room, he grabbed his tennis bag. She followed. They jumped on their bikes and rode off to Bloomington Park.

The City of Della is known for its downtown historical features and vibrant family life. Main Street, located between two lakes, East and West Lake, features small quaint shops and amusing amenities. Memorial Highway passes through the city's south side, providing convenient passage to the region. Bloomington Park is situated on the west side of West Lake. Next to the park is Della High School, home of the Della Cougars. Woods and mountains gradually rise north of both lakes. Millions of visitors from adjoining communities watch Della's Fourth of July parade yearly. At dusk, fireworks launched from West Lake could be viewed from Bloomington Park. Theo, Elliot, and Ella live a few blocks south of Bloomington Park between West Lake and Memorial Highway.

After a few tennis games, they stopped to take a break on a park bench. Theo won both games even though Ella kept the score close. She looked over at the playground. Several kids slid and jumped on the playground equipment. Sitting on benches along the play area, mothers chatted, keeping in touch on this beautiful spring day. As Theo and Ella began talking about their week at school, she decided to tell him.

"Theo, I'm late. I think I'm pregnant," Ella said as she looked straight into his brown eyes.

He stood straight up and said, "You're what?"

"You heard me. I'm pregnant. I plan to see my ob-gyn next week to take pregnancy tests. But I am certain that I am pregnant."

He was upset. It was a good thing his tennis racket wasn't within his reach. He would have decapitated the tennis racket. "I love you. I do. But I am not ready for this. We are not ready for this!" he said.

"It doesn't matter if we are ready for this. I'm pregnant, and we are having a baby."

"It's a fetus," he said, making her mad.

They kept arguing. He would talk about abortion. She would talk about the long-term memory of killing an innocent child. He would talk about a lack of money. She would tell him they would find a way to pay the bills. The pacing, back and forth, continued for a half hour. He claimed it was her problem. She apologized but told him he had to care. He wanted kids, but not yet. She would tell him they were old enough. He wanted to be with her but wasn't ready for marriage. She was. He was. 'He was not ready yet,' she thought as she started to cry. Still upset, he took off on his bike, heading home, leaving her on the park bench. She watched as the tires on his bike kept turning in the wrong direction. 'I am over here,' she thought while crying. When she reached home, all her romance novels had to be tossed in the trash can. Their fairy tales were untrue. Their stories were unreal. Today and this conversation did not happen. Then, she heard a kid screaming. She looked up. By the playground slide, a young boy with a scratched knee ran to his mother. The mother grabbed him into her arms, hugging him as she sat him on her lap. The mother wiped it clean and gently placed a small bandage on the scratch. With one last hug, he heard, "Go play." He took off with a burst of energy, heading straight back to the slide. She loved watching kids as innocent and energetic as they were. She decided that she loved her kid, her baby, and her fetus. She continued watching the kids playing on the playground. After a while, she picked up her bike and headed home to her mother. She hadn't planned for this pregnancy. It wasn't what either she or Theo wanted at this point in their life. However, it was real, and it was theirs. She had a hundred questions that needed answers and a hundred things to do before its birth. Right now, these questions aren't important. She loved her kid, and that's all that mattered.

Chapter 2

A couple of days later, Ella sat uncomfortably in the obstetrician-gynecologist's (ob-gyn) office, scanning the room. The waiting area was surrounded by cream-colored chairs and small glass tables cluttered with magazines. Brochure stands containing abortion and pregnancy pamphlets hung on the side wall. Some of the brochures were bright and colorful, begging to be browsed. She thought about plucking a few out of the stand so she would have something to read later in the day. She had visited this office before but not for this reason. She remembered her first visit to this office. Being nervous, she followed her mother's footsteps through those doors. She wondered what to ask and whether to ask it.

A muffled whimper came from the side of the room. Several chairs in the room were filled with women of different ages. She didn't recognize anybody. Another whimper spread through the room. Looking in that direction, she noticed one of the young ladies grabbing a tissue. She wondered why she was starting to cry. Then she knew. 'Why does anybody cry in this office?' she thought. Ella didn't dare start a conversation with her.

She was probably pregnant and heading for that procedure. That hated procedure called abortion. While Ella felt sorry for her, Ella ignored the noise. Ella knew why she was sitting in this seat. She was late, over seven weeks late. She was a junior in high school, and she was pregnant. None of her friends had been through this yet, and she had too many questions to ask. All of them were important. As a door opened, a nurse appeared.

"Ella," a nurse said, looking around the room. Ella acknowledged with a smile while heading for the open door.

She was escorted to the bathroom to take a pregnancy test. Afterward, she waited in the exam room for the doctor. The empty counter and new cabinets were shiny and clean. The nurse knocked on the door and walked in. She asked, "We need some blood for another test." The nurse drew blood from her arm and left, closing the door. She was again waiting in the exam room, wondering. She checked twice already at home. Both tests gave her the same result, positive. She couldn't believe that she was this young and pregnant. Her mom told her to talk to the doctor anyway. Signs were hanging on the wall. The 'Adoption is the better Option' sign stood out with a mother holding a cute little newborn. One other sign showed the anatomy of a woman and a fetus at different stages of the pregnancy. On the other wall was a 'Stay Healthy' sign.

The doctor walked in smiling, "Congratulations. Your pregnant." The words stuck like a wad of gum to the bottom of a park bench. All the noises next door did not matter as the deepest parts of her heart pounded with excitement. This was the best day of her life. She smiled back at the doctor, knowing she would never forget this moment. He continued, "You are the luckiest woman on the planet. Who is the lucky guy?"

She said, "Theodore Bharnes. I have lots of questions to ask, and I am not sure where to start."

"Let's start with, are you married?" the doctor asked.

"No, and we are arguing."

"About the pregnancy?"

"Yes. Theo wants an abortion. He says he is not ready for a kid and that I goofed. But I love this kid. I want to have a family starting with this one."

"That is a problem. You will need to work that out with Theo. Do you know a counselor? Or would you like to see a professional?"

"Enzo is my school counselor," she responded.

He agreed that she could have Enzo answer some of her questions. If she needed additional counseling, he would help her with referrals. He gave her a complete physical and reviewed the blood and urine results confirming that she was healthy. He asked her to buy a book on pregnancy and to register for La Mas classes. They talked about pregnancy stages and the delivery date. 'The countdown had begun,' she thought. He warned her about smoking and drinking during the pregnancy.

"The first month is the hardest. If there are any complications, schedule another appointment. Otherwise, I will see you in a few months for the first ultrasound."

"Ok," she said, leaving the office smiling while thinking about her baby's first picture.

Chapter 3

Enzo slid his office keys back into his front pocket. As he looked around his office, he noticed all the class schedules piled up on the edge of his desk. They had accumulated over the past few days and were waiting to fall on the floor. Some were deviations from Educational Development Plans (EDP). EDPs were school schedules for students that followed a common path of classes through their high school years. Some students tactfully selected classes to attain a college degree. Other students picked classes that lead to a technical degree or certificate. While others would only take the minimum core graduation classes. The stack of schedules next to the EDPs was Individual Education Plans (IEP). IEPs were for students that needed more time, attention, and help with their learning. Other IEPs were for students that had an excessive number of absences. Enzo had plenty of work at Della High School. Elective classes for the next semester were full. Some of next year's senior schedules were missing classes required for graduation. Then, he had to sort out the new transfer students' classes. He put his coffee mug in the microwave, shut the door, and started the microwave like his day.

About halfway through his first cup of coffee, he heard a knock on the door. "Come in," he said. Ella opened the door walking in. Her hair was shiny black and curled. She was wearing an orange and black Della sweatshirt with tight black leggings.

Staring at him with her dark brown eyes, she said, "Do you have a few minutes?"

He responded, "I sure do. Are you going to help me with these schedules?" He swirled the coffee in the mug. As it neared the top of the mug, it looked like a whirlpool almost spilling on the schedules. He let it settle, and he took another sip.

"You want me to help you with those?" Ella said while sitting down. She explained her great news and her ob-gyn office visit.

"Well, congratulations. I couldn't be happier for you and ____," Enzo said. While he had seen them together in the hallway, he forgot his name. "Who is the father again?"

"Oh, It's Theo. Theodore Bharnes," she replied as she smiled. She explained how Theo was upset, blaming her for the pregnancy.

"How upset was he?" Enzo said as he wrote their names down on a piece of paper. "Did he hit you? Did he hurt you?"

"No. We were only arguing. But he isn't happy."

"Well, don't let him back out. You're a team, Ella, Theo, and your baby," he pointed at the fetus. "Bring him in here tomorrow. We'll hear his side of this story."

"Ok." She left, leaving the door open, happy she had someone to talk to.

Chapter 4

Theo ignored Ella and the pregnancy topic for the rest of the weekend. He was trying to ignore it for the rest of his life. At school, he avoided Ella. Unfortunately, Ella saw him dashing in and out of the classroom doorways, hiding from her. She played the game early in the week, running after him whenever she saw him. After talking to Enzo, she had to stop him before his last class on Wednesday. She said, "We have to talk to Enzo tomorrow after school."

He agreed with a simple "Ok."

After school, Theo was playing *Hillside Warriors* with Elliot. "Elliot, we need to wipe out the guardians on the walls," Theo said. His player was lying on top of one of the hillsides staring through a scope. He could see movement along the top of the walls and in the corner towers. One guardian was sitting on the pinnacle of the tower. It was an easy shot for Theo. Dead. The guardian slid down the tower into the moat. "Theo one. Guardians none," he told Elliot. Extra castle guardians were now running to Theo and Elliot's side of the castle. A little expert marksmanship and Theo took them down one at a time. Elliot was bagging about as many. "We need a scoreboard. I bet I'm ahead?" Theo said.

"Ah, no. You're not," Elliot replied. The rock in front of them was taking the brunt of the backfire when there was a bang. Elliot got hit. "Not again." He had to wait on the home page for his player to revive.

"Hurry up. They are starting to run towards me," Theo blared over their internet phone connection.

"Keep taking them out," Elliot blared back.

"I think I got them all. I'm heading into the fort," Theo said as his warrior ran towards the drawbridge. He made it inside the fort hiding behind a pillar.

"I'm in. You will need to come through the front gate. You shouldn't have any problems," Theo said as Elliot's warrior was heading back to the fort. When Elliot's warrior crossed the drawbridge, Theo had already searched several towers for gold.

Elliot said, "I bet it's in the dungeon below the fort. I'll check there."

"I'll follow you," Theo replied.

Right beyond the door of the dungeon was a heap of gold. "We're rich," Elliot said, "I'm going to buy a new sniper rifle, the semi-automatic type."

"I'm got to buy a new armored vest," Theo said as his warrior grabbed the gold. "I've got to go."

Elliot knew him too well. "So, what are you doing? Studying Ella?"

"No. No. We're fighting right now. I'll explain later," Theo said, hanging up the connection and logging out. He wasn't ready for any of this. He didn't even want Elliot, his best friend, to know. He lay in bed thinking about what he would say to Enzo and Ella at tomorrow's meeting. He loved Ella. Ella was head turner on the outside. A ten in beauty and tenacious in personality. It would take his best words to convince her to have an abortion. He decided to repeat their argument in the park, hoping he would win. He checked his phone. Several texts were from Ella asking him to call her. A couple of texts were from Elliot, wondering why he wasn't back in the game. He ignored all of them. Exhausted, he fell right to sleep.

Chapter 5

Enzo strolled into his office the next day, gazing at the EDPs and IEPs still piled on the corner of his desk. While he had made some progress the day before, the stacks still looked at the floor. He was preoccupied with his appointment with Ella and Theo. The schedules would have to wait. He stared at the baseball lamp on his short bookcase. The lamp was made of five baseballs stacked on each other with an old dusty off-white lampshade above them. His wife bought it from a thrift shop several years ago. He turned it on, brightening the baseball trophies next to it. It was only a week till baseball practices started. His summer employment was coaching the baseball team. He pulled an old college notebook off of the bookshelf. It contained notes that he had taken while working on his degree. He turned to a page with the heading ATTRIBUTES OF A GOOD RELATIONSHIP.

The first attribute was PHYSICAL: RACE, AGE, SHAPE, LOOKS… Thumbing through his notes, he wondered if any of these attributes mattered. He decided he needed something to stare at while he prepared for the meeting. Turning on the computer and logging in, he searched for Theo's and Ella's school profiles. Both of them were from the same race. Both were juniors in high school about the same age. Both were skinny. Theo was six feet tall. Ella was five feet seven inches. Their stature looked about the same. She had long shiny black hair. He had dark brown hair. His hair grew straight down then it curled outward at his ears. Both had brown eyes. He smiled as he thought, 'Almost a perfect match.'

The second attribute he noted in his college notebook was INTELLECT: EXTROVERT, INTROVERT, AND CONTINUITY OF CONVERSATION. According to their school profiles, they lived a few blocks from each other, sharing the same bus stop. Both were talkers. He remembered seeing them in the hallway several times, holding hands. He didn't know much about them, but if they had been together for a while, they would've had many meaningful conversations with several stories to tell.

The third attribute was SPIRITUALITY: CHRISTIANITY, MUSLIM, BUDDHISM, ... Uncommon traditions would have raised red flags early in the relationship. He guessed that they had a common set of beliefs and traditions. He wasn't worried about this attribute either.

The last attribute he noted was MATURITY: TRUST, EMOTIONAL, RESPECT... 'Now, this is something they needed to work on,' he thought. Yes, they were too young, but then again, they were almost eighteen. They weren't thirty. They weren't fourteen. If they were arguing, one of them would have to give in while the other remained sensitive to the other's needs.

He made another cup of coffee, continuing on the next page of his college notebook. Its heading was HOW TO GROW A RELATIONSHIP. He read for a while, keeping busy with some of the intricate parts of his notes. The first noted topic was COMMUNICATION, COMMUNICATION, AND COMMUNICATION. He had pages of examples of when to speak and when to listen. He thought about each one, almost adding a few notes to the page from his marriage. The next topic was REACTING TO THE ONE SPEAKING WHILE RESPECTING THE PERSON'S COMMUNICATED GOALS. He had written 'vertical component' in the margins of his notes. As a person speaks, they need to be careful not to speak down to a person. These examples were equally interesting. Some of them were too smart. The third topic was BUILDING TRUST IN THE RELATIONSHIP. In this margin, he had written 'horizontal component.' The couple must know each other's strengths and weaknesses while working to achieve common family goals. The words, 'Stand by them. Not under them.' was bolded in his notes. The last topic was DEALING WITH MISTAKES. Everybody makes mistakes. How each person deals with the mistakes can build or destroy the relationship. In this margin, he had written, 'crooked line.' He was ready to turn the page when Theo and Ella entered his office.

"Well, good afternoon, you two. I am glad you came by," Enzo said as they sat across from him. "Ella stopped by yesterday. She said you weren't happy with her pregnancy."

"I'm mad at her. At first, I thought she was joking. You know, this was like some Halloween prank in the middle of May to scare me. Then she keeps repeating it. 'We're having a baby! We're having a baby! ... I'm too young to have a kid. I don't have a place for us to live. I need a job and a car. I don't have any money. I don't want a kid right now. I want her to take care of it. She forgot to take the pill. She admits to not taking the pill and wants me to be responsible for her mistake. This isn't happening. No matter how angry she gets, she has to take care of it. She has to decide when to get an abortion."

"Is that what you want?" Enzo asked Theo.

"Yes! That's what I want."

Both of their eyes locked. Enzo stared directly into the boy's brown eyes for what seemed to Enzo to be an eternity. The boy's curls were almost shooting fire out of the side of his head. Enzo finally looked away towards the picture on the wall behind them. It was a picture of his footprint tracks coming out of West Lake. The tracks were heading straight for the camera with the lake and downtown Della in the background. He took the picture several summers ago after swimming across West Lake. He was soaking wet and relaxing on the sand. It was a long swim and an accomplishment he was proud of. He remembered it like it was yesterday. He wondered why he had taken this meeting today. He was busy enough the way it was. Maybe these two needed to see a professional instead of him. A locker banged in the hallway catching his attention. He recognized that while only a few seconds had ticked off the clock, time was flying by like a flyball to the outfield. Enzo's glove was ready and waiting. He was waiting for it to drop into his glove. Finally, he looked at Ella and asked, "And what would you like?"

Her heart didn't skip a beat as she started, "Give this kid a chance, Theo. I love this kid inside of me. I am going to keep it no matter what happens. It is my blood, my genes, my looks, my breath, and it's mine. For over a decade, I have waited for this kid. I am not about to give in to killing it. To have an abortion is not part of my dreams for me or this kid. It is not the way I was raised or brought up. I have a lot of friends and family that would be very upset right now if they knew what you just said. We have been together for over two years. We have shared many moments. We have gone to movies, sports events, and parties together. We have held hands for years. We play tennis together. We have been together so many ways that you can't just walk out of this and say, 'I don't want the product of our love.'" She looked at the baseball lamp and continued, "You need to step up to the plate. You can find a job. We can find the money to get through this. We can find a place to live. He needs to. It is more than that. You have to want to. Theo, you can't say what you just said and not think about all the good times we have had and not care about our future."

Enzo was watching this ball fly out of the ballpark. 'Homerun,' he thought as he looked at Theo. Theo was staring straight down at the floor. Some individuals stare out into the distance. Some look up. He was staring straight down. Enzo turned to Ella, winked at her, letting her know he cared, and said, "So, that's your side of the story."

"Yes," she replied.

He had waited long enough. Enzo's ears were full, and he had to unfold the road in front of these two. He stated, "So we have a problem." Probably, the understatement of the school year, but that is what he said. "Ok, now that we know both sides of this story. I need you two to calm down. Please don't be mad at each other. Keep talking with each other. This can and will be worked out. Do you agree?"

After some discussion, Theo and Ella agreed they wouldn't be mad at each other.

Enzo continued, "Secondly, I want you to find one or two friends to talk to. Ella talks to one or two friends. Theo talks to one or two friends. It would be best to talk to friends you have been with forever and understand your wants and needs. Also, tell your friends to keep this to themselves. The last thing you want is to have everybody gossiping about this. Can you do this?"

Instantaneously, Ella said, "Yes."

Theo stared at her, wondering for a moment. Then, he looked at her for another moment. He looked back at Enzo and said, "I guess."

"I will see you again next week," Enzo said, thanking them as they left together. Enzo stood at the door, watching and listening as they walked down the empty hallway, wondering if they would talk. The school day was over, and they were the only students left in school. Their footstep down the hallway sounded lonely until a floor cleaning machine turned a corner in the next hallway breaking their feet's peaceful beat.

Enzo returned to his desk and started taking notes on their discussion. He jotted down most of the couple's words, searching for the next levels. He understood both of their perspectives. After listing several related factors like frustration, love for each other, irritation, anger, trust, …, he weighed each factor with a 1 to 10 scale. One was the worst, and ten was the best. Some of the factors needed a lot of work yet. Others were decent. This wouldn't be an easy month for either of them.

A couple of note pages later, he stared out the window. His ears were back to normal as he noticed the white petals on the cherry tree outside. Some petals blew in the wind reminding him of snowflakes dropping on a cold winter day. He was glad it was warming up outside. As winter had passed, it was time for spring. He shut off his baseball lamp and closed his office door for the night.

Chapter 6

Theo and Ella walked down the hallway toward the school doors. He usually held her hand as they walked together. While she expected this, she knew he wouldn't. However, with a good gesture, he opened the school door for her to go through. They both stopped on the step outside the door. It was a beautiful spring day, and birds chirped in a distant tree.

"I thought he was going to follow us out here," Theo said.

"He's just trying to be helpful," she quickly corrected him. "Besides, we need his help."

"When I was finished talking, I wondered why he stared at the picture behind us."

"He was probably thinking about what you said. You said it so fast. He probably didn't even hear it."

"Well, he didn't say anything after I quit talking. He went straight over to you, asking you for your side of the story. I expected an argument from him."

"He's not supposed to argue with us. He listens to us, and then he helps us."

She started to text Zoee, her best friend. "Do you know who you will talk to?" she asked Theo.

"Elliot, if I talk to anybody," he said. "He's been my best friend since junior high school. I hope he doesn't tell Abby, his new girlfriend. She talks to everybody. Elliot claims that everybody in school knows about their last two dates, and he hasn't told anybody but me. Do you know her?"

She sat on the step and texted her mom, asking her to pick her up from school. "She is in some of my classes. Other than that, no. They're dating?"

"They have had two dates. Like he said, 'They have gone out for a pizza and a movie.' At least he is dating somebody again. He is happy, and that matters." He started heading for the bicycle rack. "You want to ride on the handlebars like you used to?"

Smiling, she said, "No. My Mom is picking me up in a little bit."

He unlocked his bike rolling it to the step. "Whom are you going to talk to?" he asked.

"Zoee. I just texted her that we needed to talk." She looked at her phone. "She texted me back that she is coming over tonight. She needs help with Algebra II. Are we still going to the musical tomorrow night?"

He looked into her dark brown eyes as he had done many times before. "I still think it would be better if you had an abortion," he said, hoping she would give in, knowing she wouldn't.

"That's not what I want!"

"I know, but" He looked to the west and noticed the dark clouds rolling in. "Yessss. We are still going to the musical together. I better get home before the storm gets here. I'll see you later." He left her again. Sitting on the steps of the school, she was finished crying. Her mind was set.

Chapter 7

Theo lived only a couple of blocks from school. Empowered by the dark clouds forming behind him, he put his bike in the fastest gear. The bike raced home. He wondered if Ella had been picked up before the drops started to fall. As he parked his bicycle in the garage, the clouds let loose dropping their madness on the sidewalk. He smiled as he thought, 'I made it.'

It was Thursday night. "Elliot, where are you," Theo spoke loudly into his internet phone.

Elliot responded, "Where were you?"

"I had to stay after school for a counselor meeting."

"No. No. Where are you on these hills of *Hillside Warriors*? You know the computer game."

"I am heading back to our favorite fort," Theo said.

"No, don't. I am at a different fort. Last game, we scored all the gold from that one. So, I decided to find another fort."

"Same level?"

"Of course. My high-velocity sniper gun is blowing them away."

"Good choice. I don't mind the change in scenery. So where are you?" Theo asked.

"Right inside Fort #32. I shot the guardian. Now, I need to find a medical kit before the rest of the guardians get here. You close?"

"I'll be there in a couple of minutes."

"So, what were you doing after school?"

Theo stalled for a minute but recognized he had to tell his best friend the good news. He was still wondering how to keep the news from Abby. The last thing they needed was for her to make this into a social eruption. 'So here it goes,' he thought. "Ella and I stayed after school for a meeting with Enzo, the school counselor."

"Why? Were you in trouble?"

"Not exactly," he didn't want to lie to his friend, "Actually, sort of. But you must promise me you won't tell anybody about it. This is important. Don't even tell Abby."

"What is so important that I can't tell Abby? So, both of you are in trouble?"

It was quiet for the longest time. Theo asked, "Do you promise?"

"Ok. I won't tell Abby. But this better be good."

"Ella is pregnant."

"No! She is not." Elliot said unbelievably.

"Yes. She is pregnant," Theo said. "I told her to take care of it. I'm not ready for a kid. I don't have a home or even a car. I want her to have an abortion. Wow, that made her mad."

Elliot was even more astonished, saying, "You didn't tell her that. Tell me you didn't say that."

"No. That's what I said. I told you I don't want a kid right now."

"Get real. You don't want her to go through with an abortion. You have been together forever. You should just get married and have the kid. Both of you will graduate from high school in about a year, and then you can live together happily ever after."

"I have very little money. I don't know how we would make it. I don't even have a job. How will we go to school and keep the bills paid?"

"Does she have any money?"

"No. Definitely not."

"You still don't want to kill the kid. That would haunt you for the rest of your life. And she would be mad at you forever. Really mad at you."

"I don't want Ella crying either. But we are not ready yet, and I don't know what to do. Abortion is an easy out."

"It's just wrong. Really wrong. It would bother you. Ten years from now, you will look back and wish you hadn't. If word gets out that you two killed a kid, her friends will look down on you. They would be upset with you. Besides, you like kids. Ella likes kids. You are going to have kids eventually. Start now. Don't wait," Elliot said with an authoritative tone.

"It's not illegal to have an abortion."

Almost shouting into his phone, Elliot responded, "Are you listening? She will have many of her friends mad at you if you keep this going. Even her family would hear about it. Then they would be upset with you. Quit trying to get out of it. Love her and the baby."

At this point in the game, both had been killed by the guardians. They sat on their computer chairs, talking into their microphones. Neither one wanted to play the game with this topic hot on the microphone. It was quiet for a bit when Elliot said, "Start with the first step. Find a job."

"Well, where do I work? I'm not eighteen yet."

"Start with your resume. You remember the resume we wrote in English class last year. All you have to do is write a cover letter."

"Resume I have. Cover letter I don't have."

"I think our class wrote one last year. Let me pull mine up if I still have it."

"You kept your cover letter?"

"Yes. You are supposed to. Here it is. I remember it now." He moved the screen over to his second monitor. "We used the letter style called Application Format. It resembles an employment application form. The first paragraph was the most interesting. We had to pick the greatest event in our life and type a few lines about it. The teacher used the example of making the free throw that won the state basketball tournament or spelling the word that won the spelling contest. Then you had to follow those lines with the 'I am applying for the job of ___' sentence."

"And what was your example?"

"Remember me winning the Fourth of July boxcar race. That was my moment." Elliot almost hit the play button on the computer game, but he was enjoying this stimulating conversation and his scholastic mission. Not very often, your friend's girlfriend is pregnant. "Are you taking notes on this? You should."

"No. I'll remember it."

My work experience was in the second paragraph. I only listed a few odd and end jobs. The third paragraph was about my education and the classes I liked."

"I am starting to remember this letter. I didn't know you liked school. You are starting to sound like a teacher."

"Would you be nice? I'm trying to help you."

"I'm still listening, but now I need a notebook. I got this. Three paragraphs: free throws, lawn mowing, and industrial art class."

"Yes. You need those paragraphs and two more: a reference paragraph and a summary paragraph. Sign it, and you're done."

"References? Where am I going to get references from?"

"I quote the teacher, 'It's easier than that.' If all your uncles are in the union, you can ask them to find you a union job. If your dad owns the mall, you can start a business with his support and financial backing. If your aunts are all nurses, you can ask them for help. If your friend recommends a position, you can use their name as a reference. If you don't know where to start, all you need to do is start talking to the right people."

Theo smiled, "I wish my Dad owned the mall."

"Yes. So do I."

"I remember my cover letter now. Our format was based on Sell, Sell, and Sell. In the first paragraph, we had to explain why we liked the company, followed by the 'I am applying for the job of ____ for the following reasons:' sentence. We then had to bullet point all the reasons we would be qualified for that position. The last paragraph was a summary with my contact information."

"Do you still have it?"

"No. My bullet point reasons weren't that valuable. So, I tossed it. I should apply for a 'piss-in-a-cup position,' as my uncle calls them. They don't require any paperwork as long as you show up for work the first month."

"You mean a drug test with an application form position."

"Yes. That's a much better description of it."

"You should start on your cover letter."

Theo left the game. Remembering that his uncle worked in the construction industry, he searched online for a construction job. He found some work, but he didn't recognize any of the company names. He decided that talking to his uncle would be a lot easier. He wanted to quit searching and go back to gaming, but he decided to start writing a cover letter. He followed the format that Elliot suggested. After a few hours of typing and proofing, he attached his resume. It looked professional, and he was proud of himself.

Chapter 8

Back at the high school, a bright red minivan pulled into the parking lot as the first sprinkle started to fall. Ella jumped into the car, saying, "It's going to pour."

"How did it go?" her mother asked.

"Good." Ella was fibbing, but she didn't want her mom upset. She continued, "Enzo was helpful." She filled her mom in on the meeting and the discussion with Theo afterward.

"At least you're talking. That's important," her mom said. "There is a box on the table for you." It was pouring rain as they pulled into the driveway. Ella was wondering if Theo made it home in time when she saw Zoee sitting on the covered front porch. Zoee ran into the garage.

"Come on inside. I'll help you with your Algebra," Ella said, walking in the door and dropping her backpack by the table. "We need to talk." She picked up the box at the table and looked at it, smiling. "Here, open this."

"Is it for me?" Zoee asked as both of them headed upstairs to Ella's room.

"No. Just open it."

Zoee tore off the top tape and opened the box. She almost fainted. "No way. Tell me you're not," she said as she stared at the top book. It was a book on pregnancy and what to expect.

"Yep. I sure am."

"I don't believe it. When did you find out?"

Zoee pulled out the book and found another book under it. It was a marriage counseling book. Zoee's mouth dropped. "You are getting married too?"

"Huh, what? Not yet," Ella said, looking inside the box, "I didn't know Mom bought me this book. He is mad at me. Well, he's sort of mad at me. We have a date tomorrow night."

"Back up, Hun, and tell me the whole story."

Ella was wondering if Zoee could handle all this. So, she said, "You have to keep this quiet. Don't tell anyone. I mean it. Don't tell anyone." She began at the tennis courts and explained how Theo was upset. She explained everything thoroughly. Each detail was important, and Zoee was listening to every word.

Ella said, "Did you need help with your Algebra?"

Zoee looked at the unopened backpacks and smiled as she said, "Really? Tonight, we've got other things to study." The rest of the night, they talked and laughed. At several points in the night, Theo was verbally clobbered. As they thumbed through both books, they read some of the paragraphs. "Did you know you could determine the biological father of the fetus with DNA testing?"

"Oh, it's dad is Theo," Ella said with certainty as they skipped and hopped through the chapters checking out the pictures and reading some of the other topics.

Zoee looked up from one of the pages as she said, "Is it a boy or girl?"

"Right now, I don't know. Later in the pregnancy, they can figure it out with an ultrasound."

"You can't control gender, according to this paragraph. With meds, I mean. Do you have a name picked out?"

"Read me a few of them."

Zoee read her a long list of baby names. None of them stood out. She thought about some of the names for a minute. She needed a name that would stand out. Ella thought again when she said, "If it is a girl, I will call her Destiny."

Zoee kept looking through the book. "Are you ready to change your name to Bharnes? You will need to practice signing a curvy B."

Zoee smiled and almost started texting another friend when Ella told her to stop.

"You promised!" Ella yelled.

"Sorry. This is going to be difficult." Zoee's mom picked her up a few hours later. Her backpack was unopened.

Chapter 9

Friday night, Theo texted Ella: *Double date tonight. U, Me, Elliot, and Abby. Be ready at 6 o'clock.*

It was Friday afternoon after school. Ella was diligently studying and completing homework before the weekend transpired. She headed to the bathroom around 5:00. By 6:00, she was polished and dressed tight. A ruffled short blue jean skirt with a white t-shirt two sizes too small enhanced her non-showing tight tummy. Her mascara was exemplary. Her hair was curled and shiny. She took a last look in the mirror, twirling around before heading downstairs. 'If this doesn't knock'em him out, nothing will,' she thought to herself.

Waiting in the driveway, the other three watched her walk to the car. She looked like a model walking down the walkway. She sat next to Theo in the backseat.

"Aren't you stunning?" Theo teasingly said.

"Not bad yourself. When does the musical start?" she asked him, looking at his polo shirt and dress pants. He had showered and shaved. His brown eyes and hair curls were still attractive as ever. "Do you have the tickets to the musical?"

"7:00. The tickets are right here in my pocket. All four of them," Theo said.

"Where did you get the car, Elliot?" Ella asked.

"Borrowed it from my dad. He paid me to fill it up with gas," Elliot replied, hoping nobody would notice that he was almost broke.

The high school presented its spring theatre event, *Tangled Adoration*. It was a musical about animals in a rainforest. They pulled into the parking lot and headed into the theatre, saying "Hi" to several classmates.

Theo scrutinized the set as they sat in the middle of the theatre. It had several tall trees, a river, and wild animals painted on the walls and floor. The walls were made of plasterboard and painted with contrasting colors giving them real rainforest value. The trees and the tree house in front of it overhung the main floor of the set. The lack of support poles for the tree house caught Theo's eye. The railing in front of the trees didn't look strong enough either. As he started to laugh, thinking about what might happen, Ella elbowed him.

"Ouch," he said, "that might have hurt."

"You need to be quiet," Ella replied as Theo put his arm around her.

The brochure described the play as a rainforest musical about a few cute orangutans searching for compassion and companionship. Critics raved about the musical for its romance and sarcasm.

At the beginning of the play, two female orangutans come out and start gossiping about life in the rainforest. Worried about the rain, they start building nests in the trees. Each sang their song about life. Little orangutans help with gathering branches and leaves while looking cute and saying funny things.

At the end of the first scene, with the nests built, two male orangutans confront each other on the main stage. Theo was smiling as they fought and howled at each other in a frighting musical way. Each male declared the stage their territory. The fight ended when a tiger walked across the stage. Both males were scared and ran.

Before the next scene, Theo noticed remote control antennas being raised by a couple of students in the first row. Wondering what they were doing, he sat up straight in his chair. His curiosity was resolved when several remote-control mice and frogs ran across the stage, dodging some python snakes. The bearded pigs also sparked his interest.

With the mice finally eaten, a human poacher walked across the stage, looking for orangutans to kill. The female orangutans hid from his sight in nests and behind trees. In between his walks down the path, the females, with the help of their youngsters, sang a song of fear. The orangutans all survived, and the play ended with a cute soothing lullaby from the female orangutans who were putting their youngsters to sleep. As the lullaby ended, the stage darkened. The crowd gave it a standing ovation. Theo was also impressed and happy that he had attended.

Afterward, they drove downtown to the restaurant called Pizza and a Notebook. It was a high school hangout known for its paper-thin fries and deep-dish pizza. The restaurant had a backroom where all the high school kids gathered, talked, and ate.

After ordering food, Elliot starts a conversation with, "I'm looking for work this summer."

Ella replies, "What kind of work?"

Elliot responds, "Last summer, I was bored at home. This summer, I don't want to be bored. So, I am looking for a summer job. But I don't know what. When I find a job that I want, they always tell me 'I'm not 18 yet.'"

Abby jumps into the conversation, "My cousin had that problem. He found employment at a grocery store after looking for a job around town. He thought he had the best deal ever. But the hype only lasted a couple of weekends."

Ella asks, "Why? What happened?"

Abby responded, "They said he couldn't work in the back of the grocery because of the power equipment. He couldn't stock groceries because he wasn't 18. He ended up bagging groceries and cleaning the bathrooms. He wasn't happy."

Ella asks, "Did he quit?"

Abby says, "No, not exactly. He quit going to work because he didn't like cleaning. Then, he argued with one of the managers, and the manager told him to go home."

Elliot says, "Ya, I don't want that either. I just want to keep busy."

Abby replies, "Keeping busy is important. You want to stay involved with something and should join a sports team, band, or club. You like swimming. Try out for the swim team."

The conversation continues about Elliot joining the swim team. At one point, Theo tries to convince him to swim across West Lake. The four of them laugh as they sit at the back table, waiting for their pizza.

After dinner, Elliot takes Ella home first. Ella asks Theo, "What are you getting your mother for Mother's Day?"

Theo responds, "The same thing Elliot is giving his mother."

Elliot replies, "I doubt it. But that reminds me, I must stop by the 9 Quarters Store tomorrow to pick up a card."

Ella replies in an elated tone, "Great idea. I need to pick one up too."

Elliot pulls into Ella's driveway. Ella jumps out of the car and heads to the porch. Theo asks through the car window, "Aren't you going to invite me in?"

Looking back, she smiles and asks, "Do you want to come inside?"

"Well, I thought we should talk about the pregnancy."

"You're what! Ella, are you pregnant?" Abby's burst had enough drive to restart the car.

Abby continued talking unstopped while Ella looked at her, and then Ella stared at Theo. Theo winked at Ella and then looked at Elliot. Finally, Abby recognized that they were ignoring her and stopped talking. Theo broke the silence with, "My bad. Elliot, you best tell Abby the whole story." Walking to the porch, Theo told Ella, "I'm sorry. I meant that I need to talk to you."

Abby started talking non-stop to Elliot. She had one last phrase for Theo and Ella, "I know what a condom is!"

Elliot laughed as he started the car putting it in reverse and backing out of the driveway. Standing on the porch, Theo and Ella watched. As Elliot headed the car down the street, they could hear Abby saying, "You shouldn't laugh at me. You knew this and didn't tell me. I need to know these kinds of things…"

Chapter 10

Enzo was back in his office Monday morning after a long weekend of mowing grass and cleaning up his yard. The stack of class schedules wasn't staring at the floor anymore. They stared directly at him. He wasn't ready to work on them yet. He checked his voice messages on his office phone. He turned on his baseball lamp again. He swirled his coffee several times, seeing how close he could get it to the top. After almost spilling it on his desk calendar, he stopped and waited for the cyclone inside his cup to dissipate.

The torrent of rain this past weekend wiped the petals off the cherry tree outside his window. A small bird's nest could be seen at the top of the tree. Two birds sat bolstered in the nest, watching. He had to find names for them if they stayed around. Yesterday was Mother's Day. While thinking about the importance of mothers, he reminisced about his mother. She left him with plenty of memories before she was laid peacefully to rest. She was a talker. Oh, the stories she would tell over a coffee cup on a Saturday morning with friends and family. He also remembered the piles of laundry sitting by the wash machines and how she cared for him and his brother's needs. Common phrases she would speak were 'Only two cookies' and 'Eat your supper.' When they were looking through the oven door, she would warn them, 'Don't touch the stove. It's hot.' Several times throughout the school year, they would try to sleep in. She would wake them and tell them, 'If you don't have a fever, you are going to school.' Money wasn't plentiful either, but when they asked, she would give them a few dollars, saying, 'Remember, money doesn't grow on trees.' Before a Friday night of cruising Mainstreet, she would say, 'Be home before ten o'clock.' As they headed off to college, she would say with a hug, 'I love you. Call me when you get there.' He recognized that her never-ending love for her children made her a mother.

After organizing his baseball planner, he made schedule cards for the players, parents, and spectators. Ella knocked on his door. She was dressed in black tights and a pink blouse, slightly showing her midsection. Her hair was in a tight ponytail with a couple of small braided tails hanging down each side of her face. He asked her, "How was your weekend?"

"Look out for a gossip outburst. Theo told Abby. And she's a talker," Ella said, "she promised not to, but I bet she can't hold it in."

"Thanks for telling me. Are you ready for her to talk?" Enzo asked.

"I'm going to have to be."

"How are you and Theo doing?"

"Better. He took me to the musical this past weekend."

"And how was it?"

"I liked it. It was funny at times and interesting."

"That's good. Both you and Theo need to stop by later this week. We should talk again."

"Ok. I'll tell Theo."

Ella left. Happy that she had stopped by, Enzo returned to daydreaming about his mother's importance while working on his baseball schedules.

Chapter 11

Theo's warrior was in the watchtower, staring down into the valley, waiting for something to move. Elliot's warrior was in the lower part of the castle protecting the entrance into the fort.

"I put your name in for a silver star," Theo said with a poker face tone of voice.

"You didn't," Elliot replied.

"No, you need one. Your military tactics last night were amazing. You zig-zagged through the countryside, taking out guardians. Then, you covered me, saving my life, while I took out a few. You deserve one."

"First of all, this game doesn't give out silver stars, and secondly, it wasn't that amazing."

"I hear something on the other side of the castle. I'm checking it out," Theo said, running his warrior across the wall to the other watch tower. Bullets started flying. "Elliot, move! Move! Move! The guardians are coming in from the other side of the castle." Bullets were flying everywhere. Theo could only stay down, hoping to hold his position.

Elliot replied, "I can't move. Do you see any of the other guardians?"

"There are too many bullets flying for me to look," Theo said. After a while, he stood his warrior up anyway, sprinting him to the watchtower. He saw the general prestigiously riding on his horse. "Time for an American Revolutionary shot."

"A what?"

"Didn't you see the movie in history class? The American soldiers would tell their wives they were going out to squirrel hunt."

"They didn't."

"Well, that is what the movie said. They hid behind rocks, boulders, and trees. Some of the soldiers would hide at the top of the trees. As the English would travel down the path in their bright red coats, the soldiers in the trees would kill the general first. Then, bullets would be flying out of the bushes at the redcoats. Not seeing their enemy, the redcoats were in mass confusion, not knowing where to line up and who to shoot at."

"Oh yeah. Yep, take that shot. Kill the general. At least you watched some parts of the movie."

Theo took the shot, killing the general. "That one is dead. We are trapped, though, and I don't run."

"Talking about running. What are you and Ella going to do?"

"I don't know. She isn't going to give in, and somebody is going to have to. I don't want to lose her."

Elliot was now dead. The guardians found and killed him. Theo was picking off the guardians from the watch tower one by one, but there was a battalion of guardians.

Theo said, "You recognize we can't get married. It's a state law that individuals under eighteen are not allowed to marry."

"You can wait till your eighteen," Elliot responded. "Actually, you have a few options. Since you told me Ella was pregnant, I've been exploring the internet on the history and definition of marriage. In ancient times, you didn't need a marriage certificate to be married. They didn't have an official way of tracking marriages. By cohabitating and agreeing to live together, the couple was considered married. So, if you and Ella find a house or something and live in it together, you are married according to the ancient rules." Elliot pulled the website up on his second monitor, knowing this would be a decent argument.

"It is more complicated than that. I'm certain she is expecting a white wedding. Her friends will want to attend the wedding. Her family will be upset if we elope. I don't think that would work."

"You should have the wedding after you are eighteen. You can put the engagement ring in place now and have the wedding in a year or two."

"I hear you. What else did you read?"

"You could get married by the Rules of the Mountains."

"The what?"

"You heard me. It states that if you have carnal knowledge of a woman, you are married to her. It's that simple. And you have carnal knowledge of Ella if she's pregnant with your child. So, you are married by this rule."

"Now you have read too much. It's more complicated than that."

"Actually, it is more of a crossing-the-bridge type of thing. Once you cross the bridge, you need to head for marriage. Then you cross that bridge and keep going. The ultimate bridge to cross is to have kids. And look at that you are having a kid."

"Crossing a bridge?"

"Exactly. In cohabit marriage, some countries declare you married after two years of living together. In the Rules of the Mountains, you are married once you complete the act. In the United States, you are officially married when it's registered with the Secretary of State's office. So yes, you need to follow the crossing-the-bridge theme."

"But people get divorced," Theo said, enjoying watching his friend be too wise.

"Well, you can always turn around. At any point during dating or marriage, you can separate. But what's the point? If you love her, her kids, and her family, why would you want to turn and start from scratch? That would only make her mad at you, her family mad at you, her friends mad at you, and a bunch of community groups mad at you. And it's extremely expensive at many levels. No. You can't back out of this one," Elliot stated.

"Community groups?"

"Correct. Many community groups push for strong marriages. They expect their members to drive views on stronger marriages. They expect you to support stronger marriages once you cross that bridge in those groups. If you don't, they can get upset."

"It's not a perfect world," Theo said, continuing the argument.

"Well, it's your story. You can figure out who is upset and who is happy." Theo's warrior was now dead. It was a spectacular fight between his warrior and the guardians, but the guardians won. After reviving their warriors, Elliot and Theo played *Hillside Warriors* the rest of the night while enjoying the ongoing argument.

Chapter 12

Most of the class schedules that had been staring at Enzo were resolved. He met with the administration to discuss class sizes. They finessed the teacher's schedules to accommodate the students' elective requests for next year. He was surprised that the administration was cooperative due to the lack of teachers. However, they persevered. He talked to many of the next-year seniors. Some of their class schedules were automated expressions of nothingness, while others were assiduous to the student's goals in life. He enjoyed the conversation with them, making it a good week. With only a few more weeks till break, he was anxious for summer and his annual role as a baseball coach.

The birds in the tree outside his window repeatedly chirped the same song. Looking through the class schedules, he started thinking about the birds and the bees. He quickly recognized that it had been years since he had thought this through and that he didn't know the actual story behind the phrase. He smiled as he started guessing. Why did they use the words bird and bees and the grouping of words, for that matter? It was something to think about as he worked on the class schedules. It wasn't about color. Birds come in all different colors. Bees are black with yellow stripes. Hornets are all black. It wasn't about shape. Birds can be tiny, like a hummingbird, and very large, like an ostrich. Bee's shapes aren't all the same, but they don't vary as much as birds. Wings are different too. Eagles have very long wingspans. Bees have very short wing spans. Based on the wing span to weight ratio, it is surprising that bees can fly. Their housing is different. Their relationships are different. Bees kill their husbands. Birds stay with their mates for life. Birds eat in the morning. Bees eat all day. Birds sit on a wire while bees buzz around in circles staying busy all day. Attitudes are different too. A train rolls through the woods, disturbing the peace. Bees will go right after it. They will all go right after it. Birds fly away, squawking and complaining. He had to quit thinking about this before he started laughing again. It's probably just a biology classification thing. Birds are birds, and bees are insects. He didn't know, so he decided to look it up on the internet the next time he wondered about it.

As the school day ended with a series of loud bells, Ella and Theo appeared at Enzo's door. "Have a seat," Enzo said, "How was your week? Only three more weeks left."

Ella chirped up. "Yep. Then we're seniors," she said, wondering if they would even let her in the school door with a stroller.

Theo was prepared, too, saying, "I talked to Elliot last Thursday night like you asked me to do. He couldn't believe Ella was pregnant. It was quite a surprise. We talked for a while then he gave me a few pointers about starting on my resume and cover letter."

"Oh, did he? Are you sending it to companies?" Enzo said with enthusiasm.

"I want to work with my uncle at Zero Down Construction Company. It would be summer work."

"Sounds like a good plan. The construction business is booming right now," Enzo replied.

"I am worried about expenses. Since we will be in school next fall, we will need a place to live, a car, and all the bills covered."

"I would talk to your aunts and uncles. See if they have any ideas. I think one of them has a bedroom you two could live in for a while. You could help them out, and they could help you out."

Ella was exuberant. Theo had worked on his resume and cover letter! The gamer, tennis player, bicyclist, … is now looking for a job. He was planning out the future instead of complaining and eluding it. She spoke up, "Theo, doesn't one of your uncles have a nice house? Isn't the basement almost completely furnished? Maybe we can stay there for a while."

"I thought we should start in an apartment or mobile home. But what do we do about the expenses? I don't have any money," Theo said.

"I agree. The expenses are going to be overwhelming. I would still ask your uncle. It would save us money," Ella said with subtlety.

Enzo was impressed, saying, "Excellent! Talk to your uncles. Tell them your situation. Maybe you can work something out with them. Keep heading in the right direction."

"What do I do about next year's classes?" Theo asked Enzo.

"Earlier this week, I checked your schedules. Most of your senior classes are electives. So, if you take the required classes online, you can graduate with your class next year. You can work during the week, full-time or part-time, and take classes at night. Sound like a plan?"

"That's a lot of work. But we could do that," Ella said.

"I agree with Ella. It will be a lot of work, but I don't think we have a choice anymore," Theo replied.

"To recap this meeting. You two need to talk to your uncles, asking them to help you with housing and a job. I need to print your class schedules and check if we can enroll you in an online schooling program for next semester. We should meet back here next Thursday after school. Ok?" Enzo said, concluding the meeting.

They both agreed. After thanking him for his time, they left his office. The hallways were quiet and empty except for a cleaning machine revving in a distant hallway. Theo reached over with his hand. She saw it move. Grabbing it quickly, she held it fervently as they continued walking down the hallway.

Chapter 13

As Theo sat in front of his computer this Saturday morning, his reflection stared back at him. Theo thought, 'I need a job.' He had procrastinated long enough. Like a kid not wanting to leave the playground, he had developed a unique set of strategies to avoid working. His favorite line, 'I'm not 18 yet,' had to be thrown away. He turned on the computer avoiding the *Hillside Warriors* game. He read through his resume and cover letter, correcting typos and rewording several sentences. He was nervous. He had a few lawn mowing jobs and a couple of tasks around the house listed on it. He thought about Enzo's lamp and the meeting. It was time to step up to the plate. He had his Uncle Ralph's phone number. He had to make the call. What if he's not home? What if he says no? What if I stumble over my words? He picked up the phone. It's time.

His Uncle Ralph was sitting in his living room chair. "Hello," he said.

"This is Theo, your nephew. Do you have a minute?" Theo apprehensively asked.

"Sure. What's going on?"

"I need a job for this summer, and I am wondering if I could work at your construction company."

"We are swamped right now, and the construction business is strong. Last week the manager asked for more help, and he started scheduling Saturdays. Are you in for a busy summer?"

"I'm going to need to be. I need the money, and I am looking for a permanent job."

"You said, 'You're going to need to be.' Permanent job? I don't understand."

"This is hard to explain."

"Well. We need more help. My wife and I are visiting your Uncle Asher's house tonight. He is cooking on his grill. There will be plenty of food. Why don't you and Ella come over? Bring your resume and paperwork. We can talk then."

Theo thanked him as he said, "Goodbye." He wasn't sure what Ella was doing tonight. So, he texted her, telling her not to make any other plans.

Theo borrowed his dad's car for this Saturday night's visit. He picked up Ella, who again looked stunning. She was wearing tight frayed blue jean shorts with a tight yellow t-shirt with the phrase "Narrow Rules" written across it. It reminded Theo of the notebook phrase, narrow ruled or wide ruled. Her hair was shiny and curled. He found her brown eyes staring at him.

"You ready to go?" Theo asked as she got in the car.

"And what are we talking to your Uncle about?" Ella asked. She had plans with Zoee to make a list of baby supplies.

"You know. I am asking for a summer construction job."

"Then why am I going?"

Thinking about it for a moment, he didn't know why either. "Because your cute," he finally said. Ella texted Zoee canceling her previous plans for the night.

A few miles later, Theo was pulling into Asher's driveway. The house was located downtown and nestled on the east side of the lake. The impressionistic rock garden embellished the front landscape with a palette of colorful flowers and shades of greenery. The backyard transitioned into a sandy beach. The sand and water were encased with a rocky ledge. The house exhibited a cape cod design with three dormers, a double garage, and a centralized entrance door. Located near Main Street shops and venues, it was modest compared to the mansions further north on the lake. As they walked down the footpath to the entrance, Theo thought, 'It was too extravagant.' He knocked on the door.

Asher's wife, Bonnie, met them at the door with a "Hi. Glad you two could join us for supper." They walked through the living room into the kitchen. After greetings, Ella sat by the women at the kitchen table. Theo could see his uncles on the porch. Engulfing the palatable smell of hickory, Theo sat in a lawn chair by his uncles. The flickering flames from the grill were vividly standing tall.

"So, are you a baseball fan?" Asher asked Theo. "I say baseball is all about the pitchers. You won't win any games if you don't have an outstanding roster of pitchers." Asher was looking straight at Ralph, who was smiling.

Ralph replied, "No. It's the hitters that win a baseball game. A team needs good bating percentages with a high number of RBIs. Then, you win games. A good hitter can hit off of any pitcher. What do you think, Theo?"

Theo was staring at Ralph, wondering what to say, when they all heard a significant uproar from the kitchen. "Your pregnant!" his Aunt Bonnie exuberantly exclaimed. Theo heard it and smiled. Both uncles heard it and smiled. Even the neighbors probably heard it. The two uncles stared at him.

"Well, congratulations," Ralph said.

Theo didn't miss a heartbeat and overbearingly stated, "That is why I am here. I need a job for this summer."

"Are you married?" Ralph replied.

"No. Not yet," Theo answered. He had thought about asking her, but he was, well, he wasn't ready yet. Now, he was being cornered for it, and for some reason, that didn't bother him.

"So, what are your aspirations, Theo?" Asher asked. Theo, not recognizing the word, was left staring at Asher.

"So, you need a job?" Ralph asked, helping Theo out. "Give me your paperwork. I am sure we can hire you, but first, let me talk to the construction manager."

Theo handed him his resume and cover letter. "Thanks," Theo said.

"What about a car and a house?" Asher asked.

Theo explained that if he started working while living at home, he could save some money for an apartment and a car. Theo and his uncles talked about the cost of both. Asher said, "Well, our guest room in the basement is empty right now. The basement is fully furnished. You and Ella could live downstairs until you get married and find a place on your own."

Theo didn't know what to think. Living in his uncle's basement was less than ideal, but his uncles were right. Theo didn't have the money to buy a house or pay a down payment. He didn't have many options. So, he tentatively agreed, asking, "We wouldn't be any trouble?"

"The basement has a sliding door to the outside and a stairway to the hallway by the garage. You could come and go as you want. We won't bother you, and you won't bother us," Asher said. "Do you want to take a look at it?"

As they stood up and walked through the kitchen, Theo explained it to Ella, then they followed Uncle Asher to the basement. The stairwell led to a kitchen with a bar overlooking a small living room. There was an oven and refrigerator in the kitchen. A couch and television were in the living room. A hallway at the end of the living room led to a bathroom and bedroom. The bedroom had a queen size bed and a chest of drawers. Captivating his quests, Asher guided the two through the basement, stopping at each room. Asher had been prudent in his financial affairs early in his career, and Ralph built the house for him with several extra amenities, including a finished basement.

"When our relatives up-north visit us, they stay down here. What do you think, Theo and Ella?" Asher asked.

Theo was staring at the backyard through the glass doors of the basement living room. Lucious green trees spotted the backyard. A trampoline stood empty, asking to be played with. The sun was setting in the west. Its image was reflected across the surface of the lake. This was too good to be true. "Wow, is this a gift? What do you think, Ella?" he asked as their eyes met.

"I like it. I'm all in," Ella said and smiled. 'I'm in too,' Theo thought, but he didn't dare say it.

"Just call me when you are ready to move," Asher said. They all headed back upstairs. They ate supper, and the conversation flowed for the rest of the night. Theo thought, 'It is the best pitcher that wins the game.'

Chapter 14

On a beautiful spring Monday morning, Ella decided to ride her bike to school. She passed trees that were turning green and flowers that were starting to open in the sunshine. 'It was going to be her day,' she thought, 'mother nature was giving her the green light.'

As she put her bike in the bike rack, Allison, her friend, pulled up on her bicycle. "How was your weekend?" Allison asked.

"We went to the school musical with Abby and Elliot," Ella said as they walked into school. They stopped in the hallway by their lockers. "We went to Pizza and Notebook afterward."

Allison looked at Ella, saying, "I had to stay home. Mom didn't have the money for me to go, as she said, 'fooling around' this weekend."

Ella feeling the moment, knew it was time. "Theo goofed, too," Ella said. "He told Abby that I was pregnant."

Allison screamed, "You're what?" The shrieking scream aroused everyone's attention. Ella's eardrums were ringing while students' glares were piercing the air. Her good news was going to spread quickly. Good or bad, it was started. She was glad that she was the one that started it.

"Yep. I'm pregnant," Ella responded.

"No way. Do you know who?" Ivy asked.

Allison saved her by saying, "Da. She has been dating Theo forever."

"But they aren't married," Ivy said, looking her over. "You don't show it either."

Ella said, "I've been reading my pregnancy book that my mom bought. It says I'll start showing around the beginning of the second trimester." She thought about it for a moment. "Sometime this summer, I'll have a bump."

Ivy looked at her and said, "We have morals around here. You two have to be married before you are pregnant."

Theo was walking into school when he noticed Ella standing in the hallway next to a bunch of her friends. Her back was to him. She was wearing a short black leather skirt. Above it was a tight white t-shirt and a black halter top leather vest. Her hair was in a ponytail hanging over the back of her vest. He was wondering why she was dressed in black leather. When he heard, "Aren't you the lucky guy?" Ivy said, staring straight at him.

"Would you shut up?" Theo yelled, hoping she would quit recognizing that she wasn't going to. It was quiet for a minute, but none of Ella's friends agreed with Theo. They needed to know everything.

"So, girlfriend, when will the baby be born?" Piper asked.

Having studied it last night, Ella knew it was thirty-eight weeks from conception to birth. Prom night was in the middle of April. "I'm due the first week of January," Ella said.

Another shrieking scream came out of Allison's mouth, "A new year's baby!" 'Now everybody knew,' Ella thought. Even Theo turned around when he heard the scream.

Abby stared at her, saying, "We need to shop, honey." Ella agreed. By now, many girlfriends were gathered around Ella. She was answering the same questions. Glowing with attention, she was enjoying her moment in the spotlight. The attention would last about a week, and she was absorbing all the good vibes. One of the questions from Ivy bothered her, though, 'Aren't you supposed to wait till you get married?' While she ignored the question and answered someone else's question, she hoped her reputation wouldn't be sullied by the effects of her having a child while in high school. The question stuck. Ivy was right, of course. We should have waited.

Chapter 15

It was Monday morning in Enzo's office too. Enzo turned on his baseball lamp. It was the second to last week of school for seniors. Their final exams were scheduled for next week. Graduation was on the following Saturday. It had been a busy month, and he was ready for summer.

It was going to be a nice beautiful day outside. He opened the window of his office, letting some fresh air in. He sat down and started organizing the baseball paperwork for this summer. Twice a week, he was coaching baseball practice. The team was starting to look like a team. Fielders, infielders, pitchers, and the line-up were maturing. He filled in his planner with baseball game dates and locations.

Ella walked in the door. Enzo noticed her leather outfit and her tight white t-shirt. He was glad her skirt was thigh-length. If it had been any shorter, she would have been in trouble. He asked her, "Did you have a fun weekend?"

She responded, "The weekend was fine. Theo and I went to his Uncle Asher's house Saturday night for dinner. The rest of the weekend, I stayed busy with housework. Mom and I talked for a while, and I started reading my book on pregnancy."

"That's good."

"The reason I stopped by is to tell you that I started the pregnancy outburst this morning at school," she said, acting proud of it.

"You started it? You are going to wish you hadn't."

"I decided if anybody were going to start this rumor, it would be me."

"Ella, it's your story. Be careful."

She held a few plastic flowers and a yellow vase in her hand. "I made this in pottery class. It was one of my assignments this past semester. I want to give it to you."

"Oh. That's not necessary."

"No. I insist. You have been very kind and helpful the last couple of weeks. I want you to have them."

She put the plastic flowers in the vase and handed them to him. Enzo smiled as he took it and studied it. It was a tall yellow clay vase with defined green lines spiraling up to the top. Three light purple geraniums branched out of the vase. He decided he liked it as he set it next to the trophies on his cabinet and said, "It brightens the room. Thank you."

Chapter 16

Abby called Ella after school, "We have to talk. During your moment this morning, I noticed you had split ends. I need to trim them." Ella knew that wasn't the reason for Abby's phone call, but Ella wasn't busy and told Abby to come over.

Within minutes, Abby was walking into Ella's house. "Abby, how was your weekend?" Ella said, knowing she had a date with Elliot.

"It was another; how does Elliot say it, 'pizza and movie weekend?' Since his parents were gone, we went to his house," Abby said as she smiled.

Ella looked directly into her eyes and said, "Thanks for keeping quiet about my pregnancy." Ella sat in a chair as Abby pulled out her hair-cutting case from her bag. She laid it on the table and threw a cape over Ella.

"What style are you looking for today?"

"You can start with cutting off the split ends. Then I want to add two highlighted braids here and here." Ella pointed to the hair above her two temples. "I want a pink braid on my right side and a dark blue braid on my left side. So, it will be shiny black with pink and blue braids."

"I can do that. We'll start with the trim," Abby said, removing her scissors from her bag.

"What's Theo like?"

"Oh wow. I don't know where to start."

"You can start at the beginning."

Ella smiled. "We met in history class our freshman year. I sat next to him, and he always needed a pencil. So, one day I decided he couldn't have one of my pencils."

"A pencil? Is that how you met?"

"Yep. I acted like I only had one pencil. We argued about who would take notes and then decided to share the pencil. So, he would take some notes, and then I would take some notes. Both of us couldn't keep up. So, we exchanged notes afterward during study time. He told me he was a gamer, and we exchanged internet phone numbers. Later that night, we were talking online."

"So, you have been dating since your freshman year. That is close to three years."

"Right at two and a half years, off and on. We share the same bus stop. Then we started meeting at Bloomington Park to play tennis. We have been playing tennis for over a year. Elliot is his best friend, of course. Both of them are avid gamers. Some days it's hard for them to break away from it."

They continued talking about Theo's likes and dislikes. The conversation switched back and forth between Theo and Elliot. Before long, they were talking about Ella's pregnancy. Ella explained her first pregnancy conversation with Theo.

Abby said, "Does he still want you to have an abortion?"

Ella said, "I'm not having one. He either steps up to the plate, or I'm throwing him out of the game." Both of them laughed and continued talking about their boyfriends.

Abby asked, "Where will you live if you two get hitched?"

"I don't know yet."

"My Aunt Blair was lucky. After they were engaged, her father-in-law bought them a small house in the outer suburbs of Della. He picked up a foreclosure for a dime. The previous owner called it highway robbery. When her dad returned with 'I don't see any highway,' the owner sold it to him. It's a three-bedroom ranch with a finished basement and no garage. It needed substantial repairs—everything from the basement furnace to the attic insulation needed to be replaced. Being the scrutinizing penny pincher he was, he didn't fix anything leaving them with the repairs. He told them, 'The interest is your wedding gift. You can pay me back when you have the money.' They are still working on the repairs claiming it costs them more to repair the house than to rent a place in town."

"It was still free. That is quite a gift."

"Yep. Is Theo's parents rich?"

"No. They have decent jobs, but they're not rich. At least they don't have the cash to buy us a house. Theo's dad works as an electrician, and his mom is a teacher at Della Elementary. I think they spend everything they get."

"Well, how about something much cheaper, like a mobile home? My Aunt Demi lives in a mobile home. If somebody could spot you some cash for the down payment, you two could keep up with the bills. Some of the newer mobile homes south of town look nice from the road."

"I will let you write the first check, Abby," Ella said, laughing, knowing Abby lived on the south side of the lake with her wealthy parents. Abby's dad was a local dentist whom Ella's family occasionally visited.

Abby avoided the rich dad conversation as much as she could. They moved on to the highlighting as Abby finished trimming Ella's hair. Abby asked, "What about a car?"

"My mom and dad are looking at a new car. They said we could borrow theirs until we get up and running. It's a simple crossover vehicle with four doors and a hatchback. It has around 75k miles on it and is in excellent shape. They want to help us by switching cars and giving us theirs."

"Another great gift, Ella. Keep this going."

"Well, we're going to need them." The conversation changed to Ella's baby book and her pregnancy. While waiting for Ella's hair to color, they fiddled with Ella's pregnancy book. As Abby left, she said, "Later this week, we will have to buy a few new outfits for your little one." Ella agreed.

Chapter 17

It was Friday afternoon after school. Ella texted Theo: *Be ready at 6:00 sharp.*

Theo answered: *Am I in trouble?*

The response he got back: *Not yet. My mom and dad want to take you out for supper. They will pick you up at 6.*

He replied: *Ok.*

About an hour later, they were heading downtown to Oak's Grill. Theo had never been there before, but many patrons raved about it. The restaurant was known for its large grill, which occasionally caught the place on fire. Located in the middle of the seating area, the grill was about the length and width of an extended kitchen table. Around the perimeter of the building was the seating area. When they were ready to order, a customer would select their choice of pork or beef from the meat counter. Beef choices were round steaks, T-bone steaks, and sirloin steaks. For pork, they had various forms of ribs and pork chops. A customer would then cook it themselves on the oversized grill. Servers would help with the spices and cooking times. Baked potatoes and vegetables were also available. The marinated meat was thick, juicy, and delicious.

As they walked in the front door of Oak's Grill, a help-wanted sign stared at Ella. She smiled and thought about applying for the waitress position. The place was filled with hickory and mesquite smoke. Flames in the grill were roaring. She wasn't that hungry, but it smelled fantastic. Theo was studying the architecture of the building. The exterior had a historical appeal, while the interior was open and lofty. The second floor had been removed due to a fire several years ago. Pillars made of hand-cut wood heavily coated with smoke supported the elevated roof. He was hungry and ready to eat.

On the way to pick out her steak, Ella stopped one of the servers, Helen. "Are they still looking for help?" she asked. "I am searching for a summer job."

The waitress looked her over. Again, she was stunningly dressed. She wore a tight orange t-shirt cut short to show her mid-section with black tights. Her black hair was braided back with impressive pink and blue highlights. "Hun, we are always looking for help around here. The manager is here. Do you want to talk to him? He's over there talking to some of the customers." The waitress looked towards the manager.

"Thanks. I'll talk to him when he's not busy," Ella said, knowing she wasn't eighteen yet. However, she needed to work this summer.

At the table, the family was starting to return with their steaks and baked potatoes. Conversation topics varied at the table between her dad's employment, Theo starting his construction job, and Ella's pregnancy.

Ella's dad, Gil, said, "Ella tells me you are looking for a car."

Theo responds, "We will need something when the baby is born. So, I have been checking out used car websites. Do you have a favorite dealership?"

"This might be your lucky day. My wife and I are looking for a new vehicle, and we were wondering if you wanted our crossover. It has 75k miles on it, and it's in good shape. You like green cars?" Gil amicably replied.

Theo wonders briefly, then says, "How much do you want for it?"

Gill replies, "You can have it as soon as we find a new one. It's our gift to you two." Theo nodded, thanking him while not knowing what he was getting.

About halfway through their steaks, the grill owner stopped by their table and said, "Hello. My name is Graham Oakbe. I am the grill owner. How are your steaks?"

Ella said, "Fine."

"The waitress, Helen, said you were looking for work. Is that true?"

"Yes. I will be a senior in high school, and I need a job for this summer. I can work during the week or on weekends."

Theo almost choked on his steak, but nobody noticed. 'Ella, keep it going,' he thought.

Ella kept talking while the owner checked out her clothes, wondering if they were superficial. "I have a lot of experience at home cooking, cleaning, and babysitting. I love to work with people, and I can learn quickly," she said.

Her mom, Tabitha, said, "Oh, I keep her busy at home."

The owner winked at Ella's mom, and he said, "We are looking for waitresses. You will need to keep your hair tied back when you work. I don't want it to catch on fire." His number one problem at the grill. "Does the smoke bother you?"

"No, it doesn't, and I have plenty of elastic hair ties."

"Then, you should complete an application form, and I will look at it." He left their table to find an application form. Returning with one, he handed it to her and said, "Fill this in. I will call you in a couple of weeks with your schedule if we need you. Enjoy your last week of school." He went to the next table.

She completed the form while eating supper. For her signature, she started with a large cursive E for Ella and almost signed it with Theo's last name, Bharnes, having practiced the curvy B.

Chapter 18

The following day, Ella texted Theo: *I am out shopping today with Abby.*

Thinking that she didn't have any money, Theo responds: *Ok. What are you getting?*

Maternity clothes and baby clothes. Abby is buying our kid its first outfit.

Oh. Have fun. I work at my uncle's place later today. Theo texted back, wondering why he was sweating, and she was spending the money. He turned on both monitors and started playing *Hillside Warriors* with Elliot again.

After texting Theo, Ella texted Abby: *I'm leaving. See you in a little bit.*

Ella borrowed her mom and dad's car for the day. Ella wasn't new to driving but was a little nervous in the driver's seat. Her friends were even more nervous, tactfully avoiding conversations about her stop-and-go driving techniques. She reversed out of the driveway, taking off down the road and adding another set of skid marks to the pavement.

She picked up Abby and headed for Tienda Infantil[1] in downtown Della. Deciding not to test her parallel parking skills in front of the store, they parked in a public parking lot around the corner. Once in the store, they browsed through racks of baby outfits. Abby spoke, "All of these outfits are either blue or pink. Have you found anything yet?"

Ella replies, "I'm still wondering what we will need for clothing."

"Your baby is going to be a New Year's baby. You're going to need some sleepers for the winter months."

"Ok," Ella replied, leafing through the 0-to-3-month rack. Pulling several, they decided on a white outfit with a cute little purple heart embroidered on the front.

Abby looks at the outfit and says, "I like the color. If it's a boy or girl, it will be perfect." They continued leafing through the rack of infant clothes selecting a few extras jumpers.

They both headed for the cash register. The attendant, watching these teenagers closely, asks, "Hablo español?[2]"

Abby responded, "Un poco.[3] Do you speak English?"

"Si,[4]" she says while taking cash from Abby. Back in the car, Ella almost leaves another set of tread marks in the

---

[1] Spanish for: Infant Store.
[2] Spanish for: Do you speak Spanish?
[3] Spanish for: A little.
[4] Spanish for: Yes.

parking lot as they head down the main street toward the highway.

Della has two major shopping districts. The downtown area between the two lakes is known for its quaint little shops nestled tightly along Main Street, while the larger department stores are located near the main highway on the south side of town. Passing underneath the highway, she takes a right onto 8th Street. First, they stop at the 9 Quarters Store.

Abby asks, "What are you buying here?"

Ella responds, "Little stuff." Ella shops each aisle, enjoying the newborn shopping experience while filling her basket with essential baby supplies prescient to the needs of her little one. Back at the car, she drops it into gear again, taking off for the department store further down 8th Street.

Inside the department store, she begins shopping for maternity clothes. They shopped in the maternity section and then in the women's section. Ella says, after looking at the prices, "It would almost be easier and cheaper to buy clothes that are a few sizes larger than these expensive maternity outfits."

Abby agreed, saying, "It's a new year's baby. Between now and then are many summer months. You should wear something loose for the summer. You can fit into these oversized sweatshirts when it turns cold in October. You will get right through this girl. Don't you have some of these at home?"

"I have plenty of sweatshirts at home. But mom gave me a few hundred dollars for clothes, and I want to get some new outfits." They enjoyed the rest of the night walking, shopping, and talking while spending all of the money Ella's mom gave her.

Chapter 19

The beginning of the week flew by as seniors completed their final projects and prepared for graduation on Saturday. Waiting for them to leave, the juniors looked forward to being in charge of the school. Today was Thursday, the seniors' last day of school.

Ella walked into school this morning wearing black tights and one of her new pullover sweatshirts with the words 'Barbequed Gently' brailed across it. Finding Abby standing next to her locker in the junior hallway, she needed to talk, "Good morning."

Abby replied, "Hi. I like your new outfit. It looks good on you."

"It fits too. Thanks for buying some clothes this weekend. I appreciate it."

"I enjoyed it. Are you starting to take the prenatal vitamins we bought?"

"No. My stomach isn't ready yet, but I need to start taking them."

"Stomach? Why? How are you feeling?"

"Oh. I'm noticing. My morning sickness wasn't as bad as it was yesterday."

"Like, what do you mean?"

"My hormones are all over the place. Yesterday, I was nauseated and vomiting. It was a mess in the bathroom."

BANG! A locker right next to them slammed with an earth-shattering sound. In some hallways, noise doesn't propagate. However, this bang wasn't just any everyday locker bang. The wave propagated from its origin to the other side of the planet and back. Everybody down the hallway to the right had turned their head. Then Ella looked the other way. Everybody to her left was turning their head. There were even students peeking around the corner to see what happened. Ivy looked at her and said, "Grosssss! First, you and Theo needed to wait before you got pregnant. Now, you are talking about it like some trivial thing that occurs daily in this school. We have morals around here. You best straighten up and keep certain things to yourselves."

It was silent for a few minutes. Then Ivy's friend, Sofie, backed her up haughtily with, "She's right. You two can't talk about this at school." The hallway was returning to normal. Ella heard other lockers slamming loudly as the juniors echoed Ivy's bang. Abby spoke, "It's ok. It is time to go to class anyway."

The morning moved quickly as teachers reviewed final exam packets. In her elective pottery classes, she had to complete one last clay vase for her final exam. She decided to make something for the baby but didn't know what. A simple blue pencil holder would be enough if it was a boy. If it were a girl, she would make a pink flower vase. Since she didn't know the gender, she started making a taller multicolored vase. About halfway through the fourth hour, Theo texted her: *Lunch?*

She texted him back: *Of course. Don't forget about the meeting with Enzo after school.*

Do you want to go to lunch now? Meet me in front of the library. Tell them you have to use the bathroom or something.

Ok.

The library addition was cached in a hallway off one of the main hallways. They met in the small hallway leading into the library and began French kissing. A few minutes led into a few more minutes, and guess who turned the corner to go to the library, Sofie. They stopped kissing as she stared provocatively at them, saying, "That's not appropriate. You two know better." Ella didn't know which level of meaning she was talking to, but she understood.

Enzo's office was next to the library in the same hallway where they were standing. It wasn't uncommon for kids to be loitering in that area. He heard them talking and came out of his office to look. Luckily, they had stopped kissing when Sofie walked by. "You two get to class," Enzo told them.

Theo looked at him and said, "We're heading for the library to check out a couple of reading books."

As Theo and Ella headed into the library, Enzo, not believing what Theo had said, watched them. He told them, "You better find a good book."

Ella responded, "We will. See you after school."

Theo and Ella headed to the far end of the library, standing in front of the bookcase. Theo whispered, "Do you know the difference between good and great authors?"

Ella replied with a whisper, "What?"

"A good author has a book in every library. A great author has a shelf of books in every library."

Ella started laughing and said, "Shut up."

The librarian looked at them and told them to be quiet. They continued to waste time looking at books.

The loudspeaker blared, "It's time for the Senior Clap Out at Della High. With Della's finest camaraderie, please show our seniors our heartiest thanks by meeting them in the main hallways." After senior breakfast, the seniors were given final instructions for graduation, followed by the clap-out. Theo and Ella headed for the main hallway outside of the library with the other students. They clapped as the drummed march protruded through the hallway. Theo fist-bumped a few friends and head-bumped a few others. Ella hugged even more. After the hallway parade, Theo and Ella, bookless, took the scenic route through the hallways to the cafeteria.

Chapter 20

After the clap out, Enzo headed back to his office. He knew most of the seniors and was proud of their achievements. Della High graduated a mix of academia. The affluent went to prestigious universities, some local, some afar. Many other graduates continued their education at community colleges. Some signed up for military roles overseas, with which he shared a mutual perspective. The graduates understood the theme 'Stay in school.' Continuing your education helps build interpersonal and advanced skills needed in today's modern world. With a degree, graduates earn more responsibility and respect. For the rest of the school day, Enzo organized his desk, putting his baseball practice notes back in folders and sorting the baseball uniforms for this year's team.

At the end of the last hour, Theo and Ella stood again in Enzo's doorway. Enzo looked at her sweatshirt and smiled. "Exactly, what does 'Barbequed Gently' mean?"

"Oh, my sweatshirt. Yes, Abby and I went shopping Saturday morning for prenatal outfits. It's bright and a few sizes too big, of course. It means that I am full of mesquite," Ella pretentiously said.

"Did you find a couple of good books?" Enzo asked, wondering what they would say.

"We looked for a while. But the clap out stopped us. Then we headed for lunch," Theo answered, hoping his answer was convincing enough.

Enzo started the meeting with, "Ok. The first thing on the list is class schedules. I talked with the administration and some of your teachers. I explained the situation and asked them to be flexible with a 'non-school' IEP. Most of your classes already use an online classroom app for assignments. Are you familiar with this program?"

"Yes," Ella replied, "We use it daily in some of my junior classes."

"Good. Then, next year the attendance requirement will be waived for all of your and Theo's classes. You can attend classes when you can, when you're not working, when you need to take tests, ... The teachers are working with you. You understand there will be consequences if you take advantage of this and don't do your work or oblige to their authority."

Ella said, "Thank you. I understand. So, I submit my assignments online?"

"Correct. As long as you are progressing, there won't be any penalties for being late. This IEP isn't uncommon. We used it regionally during the pandemic. We also use it when students are having problems like prolonged sicknesses, excessive vacations, and other affluent reasons. As long as you are working with us and reading the assigned books, we will help you. Otherwise, you will sit across from me, explaining why you didn't keep up. Do you understand?"

They both agreed, asking additional questions about the classes and assignment logistics.

"The second item on our list today is uncles and aunts. Did you have a chance to talk to them? Did they help?"

Theo was prepared for these questions. He explained how his uncles helped them with housing and employment. They were generous, and he hoped to pay them back someday. Ella followed Theo, and she was equally prepared. She explained her interview securing employment with Oak's Grill.

"My mom and dad are giving us their car, too," Ella said.

"Really."

"It's a crossover with 75k miles on it. They are looking for a newer one."

"That was considerate. Ok. We have everything off our list from the last meeting," Enzo said, putting the list on his desk. "Is there anything else you would like to add?"

"Not right now," Ella said.

Enzo scribbled his phone number on the back of two business cards. "This summer, if anything goes wrong. Call me at home. I will gladly help," Enzo said, handing them the business cards. Theo and Ella thanked him, telling him how helpful he had been this past month. Ella gave Enzo a final hug as they left his office.

Looking through his notes from the first meeting, all of the loose ends were tied up, and they were heading in the right direction. It took us four weeks and some odd number of days. They would be happy if they followed through and didn't get caught in relationship snags. He was optimistic. He was even happier knowing that there were going to give the kid a chance.

Chapter 21

Sweat was gathering on Theo's forehead as he sat on the lawnmower at his uncle's house. On the first hot Saturday afternoon in June, he was bareback and generously being paid. Last week, he pulled weeds in their flower beds. Elliot asked him to play *Hillside Warriors*, but Theo needed the money, so he declined. He was soaking wet when his uncle brought him a bottle of water. Theo put the lawn mower in park and shut off the engine. His uncle stared at him as he gulped the water, his throat feeling like a desert. When the bottle was empty, Theo said, "I was parched. Thanks for the water."

"The least I could do for your help today. I will need you for at least another three weeks. We must spray the grass, spread mulch around the trees, and rake the sand by the beach. Sometime this summer, I want to build up another couple of inches of sand along the waterfront. The sand has been eroding into the lake for the past several years. Oh, I need the shed painted too," his uncle said, thinking he needed to start a list.

Theo wasn't counting the cash yet, but he was glad he had a job. "If the basement is still available, we will take it."

"It is always available, Nephew. You can move in tomorrow."

Finished with mowing, he trimmed around the house. With the lawn pruned to perfection, he rode his bicycle home and cleaned up in the shower. He turned on his computer, hoping to play a game of *Hillside Warriors* before knock, knock, knock.

"Have you been ignoring me? I've been outside waiting. You should turn your phone on and check your texts," Ella said, walking in the door.

"Quite the opposite. I've been waiting for you," he told her as he shut off the computer. 'Oh yeah, he was waiting for me,' she thought. Theo and Ella rode their bikes to Bloomington Park for a Friday night of entertainment.

Bloomington Park is located on the west side of West Lake. When the park was built, a wide concrete bicycle trail was poured encircling the lake. Walkers, bicyclists, and inline skaters enjoy the 7-mile trail. The trail starting in Bloomington Park's parking lot, proceeds over the south dike into the downtown area. It then takes a winding path through the north woods behind the lake, followed by a downhill grade back into the parking lot. Visitors to the path enjoy the scenic views of the lake, typically stopping on the south dike and a couple of the bridges on the north side of the lake.

Ella and Theo rode their bikes around the park stopping at one of the bridges in the backwoods. The bridge spanned a short scenic pictorial waterfall called Bloomington Falls. Several patches of vivid wildflowers surrounded both sides of the bridge. On one side of the bridge, steps led down to an overlook tier. Plateaus of flower beds filled with blooming peonies and pansies brightened the other side of the steps. The gardens were maintained by a local women's club that kept the gardens impressively weedless. Ella and Theo sat on the bottom concrete landing hanging their feet in the water.

"The flowers are very colorful today," Ella said, pointing to the wildflowers across the waterway.

"That they are. I was thinking about taking my senior pictures here. What do you think?" Theo asked.

"You could," Ella replied.

"Why don't we take them now," he said, smiling.

Ella grabbed her camera and started taking pictures as Theo posed in front of the falls. Some pictures were playful. Others were serious. Several portraits later, they stopped and put their feet back in the water. Ella showed Theo the photographs that she had just taken. Picking out one picture, Theo jokingly asked Ella, "Do you think this one will win some girl's heart?"

Ella leaned toward him, kissing his cheek, saying, "You already got me, honey. You don't need another one."

"True," he said, happy she was still beside him. "Did you ever hear the salmon tale about these falls?"

"Oh, tell me."

"Back in the early days when this bridge was first built. Fishermen would come out to the falls to fish. They would watch salmon jumping over the falls. Some would make it. Others would jump too high, hitting the side of the wooden bridge," Theo said, pointing to the bridge's side. "That's why all those dents are in the side of the bridge." Ella didn't believe him, but she was enjoying the conversation. "After hitting the side of the bridge, the fish would fall back into the water." He was now pointing to the water below the falls. "Taking a longer run, they would jump higher, trying to go over the bridge. Some would make it. Most would land on the bike path up above. Fishermen started complaining that this was unsafe for the bicyclist, walkers, and such. One complainer even contacted an environmental group complaining that the bridge design created an inhumane death for the fish. The complaints became such a big deal that the city almost added a net to this side of the bridge. The jumping fish would hit the net and fall back into the water. Unfortunately, the town didn't have sufficient funds for such bridge improvements. So, instead, the town decided to put up 'Beware of Flying Fish' signs on both sides of the bridge. Did you notice the signs?"

Ella was doing her best to keep from laughing, but this was too much. She had to help him out. So, she quickly flicked her toes out of the water, saying, "Ouch! I think one of those salmon just bit me. Can you kiss my sore toe?" Theo studied her toes, almost flipping both of them into the water. After they decided that her toes weren't bruised, they started up the steps. On one of the middle steps, Theo stopped her, pointing to some bees and a hummingbird helping out the flowers. Crossing the bridge, she smiled, only finding one sign, 'Don't Pick the Flowers.'

Their next stop was at the beach. Again, they took off their shoes and walked in the sand hand-in-hand. Several of their classmates were sitting by the lakeside. A football game of three-on-three was started, and before long, Theo was bareback, sweating, and throwing a football.

Afterward, they found Elliot and Abby on the beach. All four sat on two beach blankets, talking and letting the wind blow through their hair as the water lapped onto the sand. Theo and Elliot skipped a few rocks across the water while Ella noticed the ripple effect. As the rock bounced across the water, a simple wave encircled the bounce. A second wave formed. Then another. Each diameter was a little larger than the first. She was the first to be pregnant in her class and the first one planning to have a kid. She felt like the first wave of many more to come. All four of them talked and laughed. Theo pointed to his uncle's house across the lake. "That's my uncle's house over there," he said. They noticed the lights were on and talked about how helpful his uncle was.

Music started blaring further down the beach. A dance party was starting to form. Theo asked, "Anybody else want to dance?" All four of them picked up their towels and headed for the party.

As the sun set, Theo told Ella, "We should go to the park bench by the tennis courts. We need to talk alone. We'll come back to Elliot and Abby in a little while." Elliot smiled, knowing that Theo had been working many extra hours recently. Theo and Ella raced to the park bench. She got there first. Sitting there, he put his arm around her, and both looked across the lawn at the playsets. Kids were running up and down the slides playing tag.

"They're having a lot of fun," Theo said.

"They sure are," she said, thinking she would be back here with her youngster in a few years.

"Do you remember a month ago when you told me you were pregnant?" he asked. "I said some things that I shouldn't have said. I have learned more than you will ever know in the past month. My life has changed in amazing ways. I cherish our little gem. I want to spend time with you and our bundle of love. You are my encouragement, my inspiration, and my motivation in life. From the deepest portions of my heart, I love you. I want to be with you and our child forever." He pulled a small ring box from his pocket and dropped to one knee.

About the Author

The author, Jeffrey Lee Vande Voort (van-de-vort), has published articles in several scientific journals. This is the author's first novel. His college education focused on engineering and teaching. His colossal fifteen-plus-page resume includes countless hours in educational institutions, automotive product development, and manufacturing. In his spare time, he enjoys reading, writing, and gaming. He is a father to three teenagers and lives with his beloved wife of over twenty years in a suburb of Detroit.

"A good pitcher is hard to beat without a team of great hitters."

- Jeff Vande Voort

Made in the USA
Monee, IL
01 March 2024